The Fire Within

by

H. Marcel Evans

authorHOUSE®

AuthorHouse™
1663 Liberty Drive, Suite 200
Bloomington, IN 47403
www.authorhouse.com
Phone: 1-800-839-8640

First published by AuthorHouse 3/19/2008

ISBN: 978-1-4343-3248-6 (sc)

Printed in the United States of America
Bloomington, Indiana

This book is printed on acid-free paper.

Cover design and printing by: Author House

DEDICATION

To my Family, my Wife Zenobia. My Children Marcelles, Robin, Randall, Ronda, Rami and Andre.

Grandchildren and their Mothers: Ayana, Alyah, Aiyah and their Mom, Deborah, Ante and her Mom Lori.

Katrina, Kloe and their Mom, Stephanie.

Also to the memory of my Loving Mother and Father Jerrell and Christian Evans. To the memory of my Loving Mother & Father in Law Loys and Juanita Childs. A special thanks to my daughter Ronda for her encouragement and support. A special thanks to my daughter in Law Deborah for her help.

Thanks to All my Family & Friends for their prayers and calls during my hospitalization and recovery.

"People don't shut others out.

They fence themselves in."

Whitney Young

CONTENTS

Author Statement

This writing is not intended to make anyone feel guilty or to arouse anger in those who are the most obvious victims of racism in the United States of America. It is intended to encourage all Americans to think about how long we as a people have allowed this sickness to divide us, prohibit our growth and eventually will destroy us, unless we take steps to eradicate racism from our society entirely. I realize that entirely is an impossible short term goal, but it should be the ultimate goal, of every American citizen, to ensure stability of our great society.

This is not a historical or statistical account of racism in America. It is just the thoughts and feelings of the writer, in hopes that those who read it will share the writers opinion that the time has come for those who benefit, and continue to perpetuate this sickness release the strangle hold on our country and allow us to flourish as the great diverse country we are. There is always great strength in unity.

I believe that racism may be the enemy that will destroy America, unless we begin to work at removing this menace from our society. One has to wonder why racism has remained and continues to be a major problem, even among young Americans. Although many real barriers have been removed, very little has been done to try and change the thinking of those in our country who perpetuate racism. There are some Americans who seem to think that their status will be deminished if everyone in the country enjoyed the same rights and privileges. This leads one to believe that this thinking is due to a lack of understanding of what racism is and the many problems that are a direct result of it. Therefore, we will explore some definitions of racism and some of the ills of our society that are a result of it. All minorities in America are victims of racism, yet none seem to be as victimized as Black Americans.

The history of racism for blacks go back to the (3/5 clause," article 1—section 2 of the Constitution, which described the Black Slave as property and equal to three-fifths of a man. Despite the assertion of the Declaration of Independence that "all men are created equal, "The constitution denied slaves their human rights. Indians were also written out of the constitution. This clause legalized institutional racism for almost one hundred years, until the 13th, 14th, and 15th amendments to the constitution which defined the black man as an equal.

Definitions

Racism refers to any theory of doctrine stating that inherited physical characteristics, such as skin color, facial features, hair texture, and the like determine behavior patterns, Personality traits, or intellectual abilities. In practice, racism typically is a claim that some human races are superior to others. This contributes to the practice of prejudice and discrimination in a society of Diverse racial groups. Institutional Racism - Institutions have great power to reward and penalize. They reward by providing career opportunities for some people and foreclosing them for others. They reward as well by the way social goods are distributed-by deciding who receives training and skills, medical care, formal education, political influence, moral support and self respect. Productive employment, fair treatment by the law. decent housing, self confidence and the promise of a secure future for self and children.

Racism is both overt and covert. Individual whites acting against individual blacks and acts by the total white community against the Black community. Overt acts by individuals, which cause death, injury or the violent destruction of property can be recorded by television cameras and sometimes observed in the process of commission. Covert racism is far more subtle, less identifiable of specific individuals committing the acts. It is no less destructive of human life it originated in the operation of established and respected forces in the society, and thus receives far less public condemnation.

Prejudice in social behavior, is a negative prejudgment of the members of a race or group, maintained in the face of facts that contradict such a judgment. A prejudiced person tends to believe that his or her own group is superior to others in intelligence, character, or behavior. Psychologists have sought the origins of prejudice in personality disorders; causative factors in the social environment; and attributes of normal thought processes. Prejudice often exists together with social institutions such as segregation, apartheid, or other forms of discrimination. It is not found among children under 3 or 4 years of age. Discrimination, in society, can be defined as the unequal treatment of equals. Another way of putting it is to say that a person is denied Equal Opportunity for reasons that are not relevant to the task at hand. Discrimination may be experienced by Ethnic Minorities—the term ethnic encompasses race and religion as well as national and cultural traditions. Discrimination may also be directed at women, old people, handicapped persons, and homosexuals.

There is a distinction between discrimination and prejudice. Discrimination is expressed in overt, concrete behavior, while prejudice is expressed in attitude. It is usually assumed that the person who discriminates does so because of prejudice, but this need not be the case; for example, a personnel manager may refuse to hire young people because of company policy rather than his or her own attitude.

In the contemporary United States, discrimination in employment can be especially damaging, but discrimination is also manifested in housing, education, and other areas. Ethnic discrimination in the United States is closely related to historic patterns of Immigration and migration. Their earlier arrivals would typically be pushed upward onto a higher economic and social level by the next wave of newcomers. Eventually, the process leads to integration, although for some groups factors such as a readily visible difference in skin color have complicated the assimilation process. The varying patterns of toleration and repression of Jews in Europe, where anti-Semitism led to the most extreme form of discrimination, genocide, complicated their integration into American society.

Efforts to combat racial discrimination and racism have figured prominently in post-world War II US history. The Civil rights movement of the 1950's and '60s won the passage of important legislation such as the Civil Rights Acts. Progress toward Integration among blacks and whites has been especially dramatic in the South. Affirmative action was designed to help correct past patterns of discrimination. Integration -

Racial integration may be defined as a social situation in which a person's skin color has no important consequence. In a racially integrated society, people associate freely, regardless of race. Cultural differences may persist, but these do not diminish any group's access to jobs, housing, the ballot box, or public services. In such a society no systematic discrimination exists against the members of a racial group.

Segregation is the opposite of integration. A segregated society is one in which members of different races rarely, if ever, come into contact with one another as equals. All aspects of daily life are separated, and contact between the races is regulated. Segregation of blacks and whites was the prevailing practice in the Civil War. Although never written into law, it was accomplished in informal custom, sometimes called de facto segregation. In the South, passing laws (Jim Crow Laws) decreeing segregation by race. This was de jure segregation.

Equal Opportunity

The term equal opportunity stands for a variety of legal doctrines and practical methods for preventing discrimination in employment, education, and housing. Its meaning has developed at the boundary between two competing concepts of equality: equality of opportunity and equality of result.

Equality of opportunity is, for the most part, not controversial. The courts and the political branches of the US government have generally embraced the idea that people should have an equal opportunity to compete, to perform, and to succeed on their merits, without being hindered by their race, sex, or other protected characteristic. Equality of result, however, has been the subject of fierce political battles and complex court litigation. Its supporters point out that discrepancies can signal subtle and pervasive discrimination that cannot effectively be rooted out by trying to eliminate particular individual instances of bias. Simply elimination intentionally of discriminatory barriers is not sufficient, supporters argue, because members of groups that have historically been victims of individual and societal discrimination do not form the unbiased social, educational, and economic situations that would permit true equality of opportunity. Critics of the equality-of-result position, however charge that it is designed to place people in jobs, schools, or housing solely on the basis of their membership in a protected group, in direct proportion to the size of the protected group in society at large, and without regard to individual merit. Neither view has entirely prevailed. Equal opportunity has taken on life in the context of efforts to reconcile these competing views in an effective and practical way.

Racism is not the same as racial prejudice; racism involves having the power to carry out systematic discriminatory practices through major institutions of the society.

In the United States, white people are the majority. Government, business, industry, unions, churches, educational and other major institutions are almost always dominated by white people. Power with racial discrimination is racism.

Paternalistic racism. Whites alone set the standards to which all people are expected to conform. These standards and decisions are made with the best of intentions, but they perpetuate the assumption that white people are superior to other races.

Racist Society Is one in which social policies, procedures, decisions habits and acts do in fact subjugate a race of people and permit another race to maintain control over them....No society will distribute social benefits in a perfect equitable way. But no society need use race as a criterion to determine who will be rewarded and who will be punished. Any nation which permits race to affect those who benefit from social policies is racist.

Blacks supported the efforts in World War II wholeheartedly, hoping that the fight against Nazi racism would help reduce racism in the united states. About ½ million blacks served overseas during that war. The war ended and no significant efforts were made to relax discrimination in employment and Jim Crow practices continued in may parts of the country, both north and south.

This is indicative of how the actions of black Americans, no matter how noble had little or no effect on their status as citizens. Being born in America and performing all the duties of a citizen, to include fighting for your country, just didn't seem to be enough. All black Americans wanted was equal opportunity, to be treated fairly and enjoy the benefits of full citizenship.

Historical Views & Comments

The first major effort by Blacks against racism was a series of court cases involving professional and graduate education. The supreme court required admission of Blacks to formerly all white schools, because separate schools for Blacks were not equal. The major case was in 1954. The case of Brown Vs. Board of Education of Topeka, Kansas. The supreme court held that separate facilities are, by their very nature, unequal. In spite of the decision, it was over ten years later before any significant integration took place in the south.

Family

The institution of racism in America historically has limited the opportunity for black males to maintain their roles as head of their households and provide for their families. Black women were able to be employed as domestics, when no jobs were available for black men. As a result more black women than white women became bread winners of their families.. This became a terrible adjustment problem for black men and caused great mental anguish to many. Some left their families in search of work in other locations. Some families were reunited and some were destroyed as a result of these separations, leaving black women with the responsibility of providing for the family. This situation also caused a large number of black men to turn to alcohol, because of the shame of not being able to provide for their families.

During the 1960's and 70's Blacks began to use political activity as a means of gaining justice and equality of opportunity. Large numbers of black Americans became registered voters. This action led to black officials being elected to government positions. The election of Blacks in government at all levels has increased since the 60's.

America was once considered as big hearted, caring and giving as a nation. Above all there was a unity that was unmatched any place in the world. In spite of our internal problems, our unity in times of crisis, made us the envy of the world. Now in the country too many have become vindictive and fragmented. There are many who think that all is well, because of the creature comforts they enjoy. They assume their status is indicative of their patriotism yet when there is a national crisis these same individuals don't seem to have a great sense of dedication and responsibility, to insure those creature comforts they enjoy so much. Those who have the most advantages seem to be the least willing to make a sacrifice for the country that make possible the great life they now enjoy. It seems that those who have less are willing to sacrifice more and most of the time they do.

Those who in the past have used personal and family influence to avoid participation in time of a crisis, are the ones who scream the loudest about patriotism and loyalty, once the crisis has passed. Many profit as a result of the crisis. One would assume that these hypocritical

American citizens would at least be in favor of fairness for all citizens and have more compassion for those who pay the full price of their citizenship. Most seem to believe that things are as they should be, and they fight hard to maintain the so called status quo.

No one is willing to accept responsibility for this terrible evil to exclude Blacks and other minorities from economic power that may lead to fairness in other areas of society.

Affirmative Action

Affirmative action is a formal effort to provide increased employment opportunities for women and ethnic minorities, to overcome past patterns of discrimination. Under the Equal Opportunity Act of 1972, most federal contractors and subcontractors, and all state governments and institutions (including universities(, and most local governments must initiate plans to increase the proportions of their female and minority employees until they are equal to the proportions existing in the available labor market.

The measures employers and institutions should take to demonstrate their compliance with the law have been the subject of controversy. Affirmative action plans that establish racial quotas were declared unconstitutional by the Supreme Court in University of California V. Bakke (1978). In 1984 and 1986 the justices ruled against upsetting seniority systems to favor minorities. In two cases in 1986, however, the court reaffirmed its support for limited use of racial preferences for minority groups (who may not personally have suffered discrimination) to redress specific job discrimination when other measures are unavailing. In 1987 the court sanctioned quota remedies in promotions in agencies with a history of "egregious" racial bias. That year too it ruled for the first time that a woman can also receive preferential treatment affirming the promotion of a woman over a slightly more qualified man. Rights advocates, however, felt that several 1989 court decisions, including one placing the burden of proof in some discrimination cases on the plaintiff, undercut affirmative action.

GENERAL COMMENTS

It seems that whenever any group makes what is considered progress by the group, there are those who believe that the so, called progress has a negative effect on another group of the society. Programs to assist women in the work place, according to some, have had negative effects on the family and marriage. There are those who argue that many women are working out of greed and not because of need. They leave their children in the care of others and without parental supervision and guidance. They argue that women divorce more readily, rather than trying to make their marriages work, and there seems to be little concern for the children involved. Many men seem to be threaten by women's success and see it as a problem in their relationship with some women, because of their attitude.

The result should be just the opposite of what some believe, there should be more positive relationships between men and women. It would seem that women who are more confident and have high self esteem, would be an ideal candidate for a positive relationship. She feels good about herself and feels that she has choice. She does not come into a relationship feeling inferior, but rather as an equal. There is still work to be done in the culture and education of both men and women, on how to adjust to the change in women's position and attitude in our society.

The limited success of black Americans has caused some white Americans to feel that the progress made by blacks has been at their expense, and this has caused some negative effect on the way Blacks and Whites relate to each other. One would think that as more blacks have access to higher education and improve their economic status, the atmosphere would be more conducive for better race relations. Instead, progress by black Americans seem to allenate the races further. Once again, what appears to be positive for one group is seen as negative for another. This indicate a need to educate ourselves on the aspirations and needs of those who are different racially and economically. We will probably find that we are more alike than we are different.

There are those who feel that any progress made by any non-white group should be limited and never equal to that of white Americans. Maybe that is why some white Americans say there is no longer a need for affirmative action. They feel that the progress made by blacks and other minorities are as much as they are willing to tolerate. The solution to the welfare problem is jobs and the key elements to jobs are education and training.

Young Americans are hoping for a brighter future, new ideas and not business as usual. Republicans blame the democrats and democrats blame the republicans for the many ills the country is facing today. Therefore no progress is being made. Both parties will still use issues of race to promote itself over the other.

We really need policies and actions that will enhance the status and future outlook for all our young people. Once they believe that they have a bright future, then young people will begin to listen when we talk to them about strong family values and morals. AA, which may lead to a reduction in crime, teenage pregnancies and other types of negative behavior.

Leaders must ascribe higher standards of conducts for themselves, if they expect others to listen to and believe their lectures on morality. A person must have credibility if they wish others to take their advice. A parent who has used drugs in the presence of their children, would have a difficult time lecturing their children on drug use, because they have lost their credibility and therefore they are not taken seriously. Young people see or hear of adults in our society committing various acts of misconduct and go on to become rich and sometimes famous as a result of their wrong doing. This creates a state of confusion for many young people.

A lack of opportunities for young people who graduate from high school and college, cause many to conclude that there are no real advantages to continuing ones education. A lack of legitimate opportunities and desperation can cause some to become involved in a criminal activity as a way of economical survival.

The time has come when we all should realize that we really live in a class society, rather than a racial one. All so called middle class and lower class Americans, regardless of race, have basically the same kind of problems. We are all trying to maintain financial security for our selves and families. When the ability to do this is jeopardized by a slow economy and unemployment, some politicians and a biased media, leads each group to believe that the other is responsible for their problems. The division is usually based on race. This type of activity only perpetuate racial disharmony.

The blame by either group is never placed where it rightfully belong; with our elected officials separating the groups on the basis of race, even though their problems continue because no one is held accountable and both groups continue to suffer without the collective sentiment of the other. Americans must remember that the country is capable of providing for all its citizens. The white population must stop believing that they are entitled to more benefits and privileges, simply because of the color of their skin. A spirit of cooperation and more fairness may allow us the opportunity of spending less of our resources on negative activity in the society. With less racism and more fairness in opportunities, there just might be less people committing crime and welfare rolls may be lessen if more people really believe that they have an equal chance for success. Those who play by the rules of society and do all the things that should result in a comfortable life are often disappointed. They avoid trouble with the law, get good grades in school, many go on to college, only to find that society is not very rewarding. Black Americans in this position still do not find equal opportunity available to them. So many others see no advantage to playing by the rules, for many of those who do, are doing no better than they are. This causes a lot of our young people to give up and lose hope.

In this society it is perceived that a certain course of action will automatically lead to a successful conclusion. However, Black Americans do not share this belief and many believe that the requirements for a meaningful livelihood are constantly being changed as a means of exclusion. It seems that regarding employment and other avenues that can lead to financial security, those in control, always find ways to exclude Black Americans and other minorities.

The gap between those at the top of the economic ladder and those at the bottom has become so wide, that those at the lower end are becoming more and more frustrated and resentful. There will always be members in any society that have less, but in America it seems that who has less is determined by race. Those who have the most seem to have no compassion for those who have less. Many even support actions that prevent these individuals from elevation of their status. Many in the upper and so called middle class seem to enjoy having a large segment of the population below their status. This is evident of the covert racism that is forever present in our society.

The concept of race as representing separate subspecies of Homo sapiens has little if any biological significance, and today many scientists reject the use of the term in the human context. In common usage, race is a socially defined term, and the definition differs from society to society. For example, many people who are socially defined as blacks in the United States, because they have one or more black ancestors, would be called whites in Brazil. The social significance of race, then, is limited to what people make of it: A society is racist to the extent that its members draw unwarranted conclusions from the physical differences between peoples.

In recent years the term racism has been at times misapplied to various related but distant social attitudes and occurrences. For example, feelings of cultural superiority based on language, religion, morality, manners, or some other aspect of culture are sometimes labeled racist, but the proper term for such feelings is Ethnocentrism. Another loose usage of the term is the notion of institutional racism—meaning any practice that results, intentionally or otherwise, in differential representation of different human groups. For example, a college entrance examination is sometimes said to be institutionally racist if it results in a low admission rate of certain minority groups, irrespective of its intention. A more appropriate usage would be to say that such a test is discriminatory in its results.

RESPONSIBILITY

The majority in the country does not want to accept responsibility for the racial climate that has been allowed to flourish. They are not willing to acknowledge that the system put in place to exclude Black Americans is the cause of many of the problems we are now faced with. Racial discrimination has caused a higher percentage of black unemployment, alcoholism, drug abuse and crime.

Black Americans have the responsibility of taking control of their lives. They must not use racism as an excuse to not be good citizens. They must make sure their children stay in school, because that is one way of gaining confidence and respect. Blacks must make it clear to white America, that all they want is fair treatment, equal opportunity and respect.

Black Americans don't hate White Americans. They hate the white racist system that no one seems to want to change. We all have the right to dislike a person or a group of people. Most minorities can tolerate that even though its unpleasant. Their real concern is with the institutionalized racism. The system that forces many to live in very bad areas with little or no hope of ever getting out. Conditions that force them to be hostile in order to survive. Many people in this situation have tried for a long time to escape with no success and have now given up. Many turn to alcohol and drugs to ease their pain. This predicament creates an atmosphere for crime and violence. White America expects Black Americans to raise law abiding, patriotic children in these dismal environments. White America tends to blame the victim and infer that it is a lack of ambition that keep blacks and other minorities in a low economic status. The reality is, whites could not overcome poverty so easily under the same conditions with a system such as racism working against them. European immigrants like to boast, "We made it, why can't they?" They seem to forget that they came at a time when the labor demanded unskilled workers. When black migrants moved into the cities they faced a technological revolution. The discrimination Europeans faced, was not based on color and they were able to assimilate into the majority group. European immigrants moved into growing cities where they could trade their votes for political favors such as work in their neighborhood which provided them jobs. Blacks did not have this political advantage. Immigrants came to this country voluntarily with their culture and family traditions in tact. Blacks came from slavery and have had to struggle just to support their families. It has been much harder for blacks to try to catch up, being trapped in ghettos and facing systematic racism. Many whites exaggerate how quickly they escaped from poverty. Many immigrants from rural backgrounds took three generations to begin to move into the middle class, and they did not have to face racial discrimination.

Yet many say blacks could do better if they wanted to. This indicates that they have no understanding of the affect racism has had on the progress or lack of progress of Black Americans.

Most white Americans seem to forget the property values in black communities were low, which meant a low tax base and that resulted in inferior schools for many years. Now after integration of schools, it is still hard to be motivated to learn and maintain an interest in school while living in extreme poverty, and struggling with an inferior basic school background. It is a known fact that for many years, schools were separate but very un equal.

RESPONSIBILITIES

Parenting

Parenting is a great Responsibility because thats where a lot of young people formulate their ideas on race. Parents should talk to their kids more about race because even if the parents are not *prejudice* kids pick up ideas about race from other kids & people and television & movie images.

There was a recent television show with very young kids who had very distinct views about race. Most all saw white persons as being smarter and better looking and less violent than people of color. Many of the young white kids 9-12 years of age saying that blacks are in gangs and they do hijackings. These kids are getting this information from some source. Often times the parents are shocked when they hear some of the things their kids say about race. Thats when parents must talk to kids about race. Many of the kids on the show I saw were saying they didn't like Jews because they killed Jesus. There was just a lot of negative information that these children received from sources that their parents did not know about. That is why its very important that parents constantly screen information that their kids are being exposed to and talk often about it. Our society has become so diverse that it is just stupid to even think about one race or ethnic group being superior to others. The division among our people that this type of thinking creates, will weaken us as a nation. It could possibly lead to our destruction as a united nation. Children should be taught that all of our citizens from all groups do the things that are considered acts of good citizens. They pay taxes they fight in wars and most teach their children to respect others.

Most of all parents want their children to be happy, and they can not be happy if they are taught to hate others who are different than themselves.

Because we live in a country that is so diverse, it does not make sense to be racist or prejudice, based on color or ethnicity.

CRIME

P oliticians do not always seek meaningful and preventive solutions to the problem of crime. Legislators pass laws to increase the time one must serve for certain crimes and allow law enforcement to arrest people for minor crimes. This gives the illusion that something is being done about crime. This way of dealing with the crime problem has caused other problems, such as overcrowding in prisons. It has also increased the problem of disparity concerning black and Hispanic Americans. Many black and hispanic people because of their economic positions live in communities where crime, violence and drug use is more rampant. There is also more police activity in these areas which leads to more black and hispanic people being arrested.

Every one should know that there are more white Americans using drugs than black and hispanic, but a smaller number of whites are arrested for drug use. This is due to the fact that many white Americans go into black and hispanic areas to purchase drugs. They then go back to their own communities to use the drugs. Areas that are not considered as areas where drug use is a problem by law enforcement. White Americans also have other ways of getting drugs and avoid arrest because many of them are not a focus of law enforcement.

The criminal justice system is such that black, hispanic and other minorities do not receive fairness in prosecution or sentencing. Getting these people off the streets, seem to be the only concern. These people are perceived to be the cause of the problem, because their activity is often time made public by the media. They are most times represented by a public defendant who is a part of and an employee of the system. Many of whom have such a heavy case load, so no one they defend gets proper attention to their case. They are there to make sure that all legal requirements and proper paper-work is done. No matter what the outcome, it is concluded that the person had a fair trial. This is not justice and fair treatment under the law, to which the constitution states that we are all entitled.

It is understandable why minorities and especially blacks and Hispanics feel they cannot get fair and just treatment in the criminal justice system. This perception by many shows why we need diversity in our legislative branch of government and at all levels of the criminal justice system. People who have a better understanding of the conditions under which certain people live, can provide insight that will lead to better and more meaningful laws being made concerning all Americans.

Everyone must accept some responsibility for racism in the country and work hard for its removal. We must begin to talk to one another about our feelings and share experiences that relate to the subject of race. Often blacks are not sure if they should talk about race with whites they are close to, and whites don't know how to respond if they do. Therefore we must be honest in our discussions even though we are uncomfortable. We should all build relationships with people different than ourselves. The relationships we have at our work-place, must be extended to some social encounters, so we can really get to know the person. The greater our understanding of others, the better our chances are of solving the problem of race. Most times our actions or reactions regarding race is based on hearsay, because we have no personal knowledge of people of other races.

Racism is a problem that affects us all and we should work together to resolve it because it is our responsibility to try to create a better country for our children. Kids in school should be taught to value diversity rather than seeing it as a negative. White America must realize that making available jobs with decent wages and benefits for blacks and other minorities, does not mean fewer jobs for white Americans.

We all must begin to think as Americans first and remove the wall that divides us and causes one group or race to blame the other for their problems. We must begin to place the blame where it rightfully belongs; be it our federal or local governments, business practices of corporate America or our selves. We are responsible for our own thoughts and beliefs and if we believe something is wrong or negative, we should strive to correct or change what ever is causing the problem. We have allowed ourselves to become conditioned to think competitively rather than cooperatively. This form of thinking has kept us from making greater progress in race relations.

EDUCATION

America faces a very serious social problem. This problem has to deal with the mis- education and under education of society's black youth. Black youths, as were blacks in the past, are caught within a destructive whirlpool of socialization. This would allow one to concede to the fact that many black youths, when born, can be correctly labeled as disadvantaged. This word disadvantaged as we know it, encompasses a broad range of conditions. For black youth, this represents deficiencies in the economic and social sense, and primarily in the area which serves as the cause of the other two; that of education.

By evaluating the past history of blacks and the education system, as well as the current status of blacks, we can more accurately determine the types of programs needed and how to make existing programs more effective. It is important to acknowledge that given the nature of the problems that black youths face, it is important to establish programs of guidance which are specifically applicable to the unique situation of this particular group. If adequate programs are not created or existing programs enhanced then the current trends will continue, and the negative effects could prove to be quite significant to society and even more detrimental to the black population.

Failure in education for blacks began the moment they entered this country. There were laws which forbade blacks learning to read and write; therefore, contact and association with whites by means of a servant status served as their earliest means of education. Blacks learned the language and acquired the culture. Some slaves however, received more opportunities to acquire knowledge than others therefore, a gap developed. This gap represented the difference between those slaves with no education to those with a small amount to those who were very educated on a relative scale. Despite this fact that some slaves did receive, informally, education from their masters for the purpose of increasing efficiency and because they were favored by their masters, for the race as a whole, education for all practical purposes was a non-existent asset. In 1860 nine-tenths of all black-American slaves were illiterate, while the remaining one-tenth maintained very insignificant amounts of education. At the onset of reconstruction, enthusiastic liberalism was primarily responsible for the establishment of church and missionary schools. However, this attempt at classical education failed. For it did not adequately meet the demands of the race. This tossed the whole notion of educating blacks into a dubious mode. Booker T. Washington created popularity for the institution of industrial schools, which was an idea which the south advocated on the lines that it maintained the status quo in keeping Blacks as servants. "Classical education would spoil these valuable servants." The north also supported the idea, feeling that it was the most practical means of dealing with what they perceived to be a hopeless situation. On the other hand, educated Blacks were opposed, believing that the design of such a program was only useful in maintaining the subjugation of the race.

Even in the 1954 Supreme court decision outlawing racial segregation in public schools did little in closing the educational gap in the south, and court orders to correct racial balance have yet to bring about quality integrated education in our inner cities. In the 1960's, poor, disadvantaged Blacks were dubbed as "culturally deprived," by many educators, and thus blamed for their failures. Minority educators objected, saying that it was the schools that were failing the students as opposed to the children failing the schools. White educators were blaming the victim while Black educators were blaming the system. None the-less, the fact remains that a seriously detrimental social problem does continue to exist. In 1970 the following stats existed; 26% of black students were two or more years below grade level as opposed to 9% whites; 22% of Blacks students dropped out of high school by age 16, 12% for whites; in 1970 56% of the Black population were high school graduates, 78% for whites; more recent stats show that 29% more Black students graduated from high school in 1982 than did in 1975; however, enrollment in college has declined by 11%. Dr. Adrienne Bailey who was vice president of Academic Affairs at the National College Entrance Examination Board, said, "there is racial cancer that is before our eyes destroying Black America-and that cancer is the rapidly escalating disintegration of minority talent in America.

Blacks are slipping in education, indicators are across the board."

In a past issue of *Black Issues in Higher Education*, Dr. Bailey provided the following: The percentage of Blacks in college prep courses in high school is significantly lower than for whites and non-college prep students do not get access to quality facilities such as science and computer laboratories; enrollment in college has declined enrollment in post-graduate degree programs has dropped consistently since 1981; Black males with post-graduate degrees has dropped while increasing for Black females; "This," she says, "poses a serious threat to Black male-female relations and could result in an educationally divided black community." Black student enrollment in teaching programs has steadily decreased such that, Blacks will represent only a very small percentage of the teaching force in the future; since 48% of Black college students are from lower-income families, they are the hardest hit by Federal reduction in financial assistant programs. More and more states are depending on performance tests to ranked and set standards for students; however, due to cultural differences and a history of poor education, Black students tend to do poorly on these tests. As the use of these tests becomes more widespread, Dr. Bailey believes that more Black students will begin to exit from the educational system. Dr. Bailey believes that the problem is not necessarily racism; however, a problem on the part of both blacks and whites in making themselves aware of the problems which Black students face. She feels that it is the responsibility of Black educators to increase their awareness in order to "restore education to a place of primacy in the Black family and the Black community."

For Blacks the establishment and implementation of programs in public schools has developed very slowly, characterized by less than adequate support and incompetent teaching. While statistics concerning the literacy of Black students have noted a reduction in the number of Blacks who are illiterate. So while the situation has improved things are still far from being perfect. Also it is important to concede that literacy is in no way synonymous to education. The public school system is definitely where the problem exists. A study conducted by Rev. Virgil C. Blum in a study of 54 private inner-city schools, indicated that Black students achievements at the private school levels were very significant. Also, cases of deviance and truancy were very low. Rev. Blum offered that a possible reason for this was the fact that since parents paid tuition at these private institutions they felt more compelled to get involved and provide support for the objectives of the instructor. Nothing in Blum's study suggested that the parents of the private-school children were any more elite than those of the public schools, only that they may be more aware of the academic needs of their children.

So where then does change began? M. Carl Holman, President of the National Urban Coalition, feels that Black youths are failing to acquire the basic fundamentals at the primary levels; kindergarten and first grade. These are the key years in the educational development of youths, and according to Mr. Holman, Black youths are neglecting to take the courses that are essential for developing the basic skills and study habits necessary to compete effectively in the areas of math and science at the higher levels of school; therefore, upon graduating

Blacks are ill-prepared to contribute to the advances of technology. As a result, Black students develop inferiority complex's, since they are unable to compete effectively with their white counterparts; therefore, fail to develop the vision of pursuing education at the levels past high school. According to Holman it is the responsibility of the Black community to become more aware and realize that the primary levels of education should serve as the arena for which to install the consciousness of, "technological survival," and, "economic self-sufficiency," in black youth.

It appears that these deficient attitudes seems to surface around the middle grades (middle school and junior high). A study conducted by three researchers; Philip Langer, John Michael Kalk, and Donald T. Searls, shows that somewhere around the junior high school level Black students begin to part with the education system. Match corporations with particular schools. Another program in Chicago the High School Renaissance Program. A program with reading, writing, and math that also provides tutoring in order students maintain their grade level. Washington DC established education camps. Involving students in computers, basic skills of math, reading and writing.

Programs to combat serious problems of the mis education and under-education of Black youths presently exists due to a spreading Black community. However, there is still much to be done. My purpose beginning with a history of Blacks and education was to compare past and current achievements and to allow the reader to realize that the condition of the Black community is not solely the fault of the Black community. However, given this, it is very important for Blacks to realize that the time has come to stop blaming White America for problems in the Black community and mobilized their response to deal with the problems most effectively. As Blacks become more conscious of their situation, they will be able to effect economic change by realizing the necessity of education. It requires the emphasis of strong values and principles of the entire community; teachers, businessmen, and politicians before real change. A thousand mile journey begins with one step, and luckily some significant steps have been made.

Governments, local and federal, have a responsibility to make education available to all its citizens. The focus should be on getting excellent performance from all our public school systems. This would insure that all our students get a good education, no matter what their economic status is.

Setting up many different school systems across the nation with no national standard, is not the way to benefit the most citizens. Those who wish to send their children to private schools, may do so at their own expense. However this should not allow them to avoid their responsibility of paying taxes to support the public school system. There are some people who seem to want a system that will provide a good education to only some of our citizens, while those who have no choice except public education, will get an inferior education. That will become another reason for division among our citizens. We should all be seeking ways of promoting quality in every aspect of our lives. This will certainly not happen if any of our children are getting an inferior education.

We must remember that we have some very good public school systems and our goal should be to improve those that are not.

WELFARE

Now there is talk about changing the welfare system. Moving people from welfare to work, sounds great and I think that most working Americans black and white approve of this. However there need to be efforts made to insure that minorities do not continue to face discrimination while seeking employment and assurance that they experience the same course of advancement in their employment as white employees. There are many who will say that discrimination no longer exist in employment today, yet one has to wonder why black American's income is still lower than white Americans with the same education and experience, often in the same organization.

Unless all citizens are willing to discard distorted beliefs and myths of people different than themselves and work toward insuring that all Americans have true equality, changing the welfare system will not have the effect that most would expect. There will be those with their perceived views of minorities, who will be happy to know that some of those lazy freeloading people are finally working. Many of these don't seem to realize that most people on welfare, don't want to be on it, they just don't know how to get off. Most people on welfare would love to really experience the American dream and become independent and productive but they live in such a state of hopeless despair, they suffer from low self esteem and self worth, they no longer dream of escape. It would be naïve to say that all welfare recipients have the desire to be productive and independent, because for many their problem of dependency is so deep that some form of deprogramming will be necessary to even begin to deal with their problem. However it is possible to change the outcome of the children of those who fall into this category.

The welfare program was an ill fated program from the beginning. It should have remained a program that assisted people who lost their jobs, on a temporary basis until reemployment, and of course children without parental support and handicap persons on a permanent basis. The program should have been designed to promote family stability, by allowing the men to remain in the home while receiving training or what ever assistance needed for employment. Instead the program requirements were that no adult male could be in the home, if a woman wanted to receive assistance for herself and children. This policy caused many men who could not find work because of discrimination, a lack of education and training and due to the changes brought on by the industrial revolution, to leave their families so their wives and children could receive the benefits. The problem of the welfare program could have been solved without too much difficulty when the number of people on welfare were very small. No one with the power to effect change, considered it to be important, because many felt that those on welfare were not the kind of people one should be overly concerned about. Since many were minority and especially blacks, who in earlier years were not allowed to vote. Therefore politicians were not concerned about problems that affected people from whom they could not get votes. Those in power failed to realize that no problem in society that only affects a certain group, can continue for very long, before it affects the society as a whole. After the voting issue was resolved and blacks were given full voting rights, the white politicians began to go after the black vote. They promised things that would not cause white voters to be upset with them. So they never sought solutions to the real problems of black people. Those in power never saw welfare as a problem because it kept blacks at a low economic level with no hope of elevating themselves, so they perpetuated the problem by improving and increasing a failing program. Payments and benefits were increased to a point that many lived better on welfare than they would had they been working menial jobs. So, many gave up on becoming employed, and accepted welfare as a way of life, rather than a means to an end. Welfare would have been a better program if we had done a lot more for those on it, if it had kept the families in tact when ever possible, provided day care for the children while the parents received education and training that would qualify them for the types of employment available. This approach would have solved two problems, one it would have made more of the parents employable, and two, it would have provided the children with structured training and social skills at an early age, which would have been a big step to begin dealing with the problem of generational welfare. After the adults received training, there should have been placement centers to assist these people in locating jobs. Businesses could have been given tax breaks or other incentives for hiring people from the placement centers. Efforts such as these would have been far less costly, and a better program than the one now in place.

The present program has created a large number of single parent families, which has made it difficult to maintain strong family values. That is not to say that all families have suffered a decline in their values while living in poverty, in an affluent society that flaunts its riches like a badge of honor. Every media of the society is saturated with images of money and power. This is constant humiliation to those living in poverty. It makes them feel like failures and contributes to a self hate image. It also creates hate and resentment for those who seem to have so much while they have so little. Many living in poverty have given up hope of ever rising above their present circumstances. Many turn to crime in an effort to overcome their condition, others turn to alcohol and drugs to deal with their state of hopelessness. All of these actions only make their situation worse.

The powers that be, with all the information about the failures of the welfare program, would still rather build more jails, than institute programs that would insure that fewer of the kids that grow up in poverty, will not turn to crime. By providing a more structured environment when the children are young would cultivate self esteem, a desire to learn and provide hope, so that fewer of these children will be prone to crime when they are older.

The welfare program in its present form, often destroy families. If you destroy the family unit, you will eventually destroy the nation. Many people don't feel a need to marry any more, even though children are involved. This deprives the children of the basic structure in their lives. Some people have a false dependency on government assistance, rather than committing to the responsibility of parenthood by both male and female. We must insure that every citizen has the opportunity to find meaningful employment. If assistance is needed it should be of a temporary nature and every effort should be made to assist in reemployment. This is not a problem that can be quick-fixed. It will take time and careful planning.

Welfare recipients do not become wealthy, they just get by. The only people who do well economically from the welfare budget are those who provide services to welfare recipients.

> We must create an atmosphere where all races
> and all cultures are recognized for their
> contributions and we all must work together
> to make our society a better place for all our citizens

Economics must be a consideration of any planning to remove people from the welfare rolls. People must be trained for jobs and there must be jobs for them or they will just become additions to the unemployment rolls. There also must be some efforts to leave certain portions of the program in place, such as health care for the children. Many of those being placed will not always acquire jobs that will enable them to pay for health care. There is also a possibility that housing may have to continue for a time, so that many won't just go from welfare to the homeless rolls. The problem of welfare did not occur over night and therefore is not a problem that can be solved with a quick fix solution.

There has been racism involved in the policy making regarding welfare because of the erroneous belief most people on welfare are black and Hispanic Americans. Policies should be an effort to insure that no American is forced to rely on welfare for basic human needs. There has always been negative portrayal of black Americans by the media. The media has caused crime and welfare to become political buzz-words. Politicians during elections have said that they were going to cut welfare and reduce crime. To bigoted white people, this meant that they were going to do something to further control the black population. these kinds of statements tend to imply that no white people commit crime and none are on welfare. It is strange that so much effort is spent on doing things to hurt and degrade a group of people who are at the bottom of the economic ladder. People who have tried so hard to be accepted in the mainstream of this society. It is very difficult for black Americans to see immigrants come into the country and right away have more privileges and benefits than they who were born here, all because of skin color. Many black Americans have fought and died for this country in every war and is still treated unfairly and is not accepted as a first class citizen.

The following is an outline of the social and welfare services as provided by Grolier Electronic Publishing, Inc.:

Copyright-1992 Grolier Electronic Publishing, Inc.

Social and Welfare Services

Public assistance programs, commonly called "welfare," provide cash or in-kind benefits for particular categories of the financially needy. Public provision for the needy in the United States remains strongly influenced by the Poor Laws of England, which were highly punitive and stigmatized recipients of public charity. US welfare programs grew significantly in the decades following World War II, but increases in welfare costs during the 1960's and '70's brought into question the extent and quality of public assistance. In the early 1980's the Reagan administration reduced welfare expenditures and suggested turning responsibility for maintaining funding levels for some welfare programs on the states themselves—and, in some cases, on the larger cities. The result has been a widening of the already existing disparities in social services spending between states, and between cities and regions within a state.

Major US Programs

The main public assistance income benefit program is aid to families with dependent children (AFDC). Three other programs are often included when welfare' is referred to: Emergency Assistant (EA), General Assistance (GA), and Supplemental Security Income (SSI). AFDC and EA are paid for by a combination of federal, state, and local funds.

GA is funded by the states and localities alone. AFDC, EA, and GA are administered by states and localities, which establish their own need standards and benefit levels. These vary widely, and as a result great disparities exist in assistance levels from state to state. The federal government funds and administers SSI, although 27 states provide additional SSI payments above the federal level. Applicants for all programs are subject to a means test, which determines eligibility according to income and assets. What may be included in assets,, however, differs among the states and across programs.

Aid to Families with Dependent Children (AFDC)
The largest and most costly of all the income welfare programs (16.5 billion in 1987), AFDC is intended to cover the minimum costs of providing care for dependent children. Such aid is available for children in need who have lost the support of a parent because of death, prolonged absence, or incapacity and for the parents or guardians with whom the children live.

First enacted in Illinois in 1911, legislation providing funds to enable widows and deserted women to care for their children had been passed in 19 other states by 1913. Aid to Dependent Children was included in the Society Security Act (1935) to serve mainly widows with children in their homes as a joint federal-state assistance program, under which the federal government provides matching grants to the states and each state administers its own program. Because no federal minimum benefit level has been established, benefits vary extensively from state to state. To qualify for AFDC in any state, children must be less than 18 years of age, or less than 19 and in high school: lack parental support; and be financially needy. Twenty-seven states provide benefits under stringent criteria when either parent is unemployed (AFDC-UP).

Supplemental Security Income

Federal-state programs funded by grants from the federal government were enacted for old-age assistance and aid to the blind as part of the Social Security Act of 1935. Aid to the Permanently and totally Disabled was enacted in 1951. In 1974, Supplemental Security Income (SSI) replaced these state-administered programs. It provides a uniform, federally administered minimum cash income to aged, blind, and disabled people. In January 1989, 4.5 million persons received SSI payments.

General Assistance

General assistance is available to people who are ineligible for federal categorical programs. Eligibility is based on state-defined need and verified by a means test that considers all income and assets, including, in some state, the possibility of aid from relatives. Benefits in 32 states range from cash payments to groceries and shelter and are administered by state or local authorities. During 1988 there were approximately 1.1 million recipients.

Emergency Assistance

In some states emergency assistance is provided for specified emergencies to adults eligible for SSI and to destitute families with children under age 21. Eligible adults must experience sudden emergencies that deprive them of the means to stay alive and healthy. Benefits are in cash, in kind, or in voucher form. Emergency assistance programs in 1988 operated in 27 states, serving about 50,000 families with an average benefit of $196 each.

Additional Programs

In addition to the four major income programs, the public assistance system also includes housing allowances; Medicaid; food stamps; school meals; welfare-to-work programs, which provide job placement, training, or public-service employment; earned-income-tax credit for low-income workers with a child in the household; and the Low Income Energy Assistance program, which applies at a minimum one supplementary fuel or utility payment during the heating season to certain public-assistance and SSI recipients and other low-income persons. Social services include daycare Centers, foster and protective care, family planning, services to the mentally retarded and drug and alcohol abusers as well as other types of in-kind assistance.

Growth and Costs

In 1960 about 800,000 families received AFDC assistance, In 1987 more than 3.7 million families were in the program, including 7.3 million children—one child in every nine under the age of 18. In 1986. $16.5 billion was spent on public assistance and$14.8 billion on SSI, which constituted 3.1% of the total federal budget and only .007% of the total 1986 gross national produce (GNP).

In 1987, AFDC families received an average monthly payment of $355 for an average annual payment of $42660 per family. The median income in 1987 for all US households was $25,986, and for four-person households, $36805—at a time when the federal government defined the poverty threshold as a cash income of $11611 for a family of four. Some 32.4 million Americans, or 13.5% of the population, were under the poverty level.

Each state has a basic—needs standard for families without income. In 1986, Vermont, with the highest need standard ($996), paid $676; Kentucky, with the lowest need standard

($246), paid $246, while Mississippi, with a need standard of $443, paid $144.

Criticisms and Reforms

Some critics charge that welfare costs are excessive, that fraud is widespread, and that welfare undermines the work ethic. Other critics argue that benefit levels are inadequate, that the system has too many inequities, that it is inefficient, and that costs are increased through overzealous surveillance and the use of means tests.

Whether it is viewed as an unnecessary drain or an inefficient necessity, however, public assistance cannot be separated from larger events in society. Since World War II the number of people on AFDC rolls has increased because of population growth, family breakdown, periods of high unemployment, the shrinkage in the number of jobs for unskilled labor, and an increase in the number of female-headed one-parent families.

In addition to the increase in the number of people on welfare, costs are also influenced by the nature of public assistance regulations themselves. In the case of AFDC, they have encouraged family separations and discourage single mothers from marrying or remarrying. When an employed recipient earns or saves more than is allowed by regulations, some or all benefits are taken away. Thus some working AFDC mothers have lost subsidized day care for their children and have had to leave their jobs.

To reform welfare, President Richard Nixon proposed (1969) the Family Assistance Plan (FAP), and President Jimmy Carter (1977) the program for Better Jobs and Income (PBJI), neither of which was enacted. Beginning in 1981 the administration of President Ronald Regan pursued several strategies with regard to the "welfare mess." It tightened eligibility requirements and reduced benefits for existing programs. AFDC eligibility requirements reduced the benefits of some employed AFDC persons to a point below what they would receive if they were unemployed. The new regulations were thus work disincentives.

The Reagan administration emphasized a "new federalism," by which it hoped federal responsibility for most social programs would devolve to the states. The states did not agree because they were uncertain of the potential costs. For several decades debate has continued regarding welfare in relation to the proper role of government, responsibilities of individuals and society, inequality, dependency, theories of causation of poverty, and the best organization of welfare.

Concurrent with the welfare debate, many democrats in Congress, civil-rights organizations, advocates for the poor, and churches urged the continuance of federally backed programs to help deprived persons. In recent years a consensus developed in Congress favoring reforms to encourage welfare recipients to find jobs and to free themselves from long-term dependence on welfare programs.

In September 1988, Congress passed a major welfare reform bill. The Act provides that single parents on welfare with children over three have to participate in a Job Opportunities and Basic Skills (JOBS) program offering education, training, and work. One adult in each two-parent welfare household would have to participate in a job search. If no work is found, he or she will be required to work 16 hours per week in a state-organized job or work toward a high school diploma. States are to concentrate resources on young parents without high school education, long-term recipients, and families with older children. JOBS participants would receive transportation, Medicaid, and child-care help for at least a year. All states are now required to pay cash benefits to two-parent welfare families. In 1988 only 27 states, the District of Columbia, and Guam did this. States are also expected to intensify child-support enforcement from noncustodial parents (including wage withholding under court-awarded rulings) through improved use of computerized systems.

The effects and results of this law—which will cost $3.34 billion for the first five years—will be seen only gradually, Congress, for example, gave the states until October 1, 1990, to put the basic welfare-to-work provision into place, so that the states can pass their own laws in order to be eligible for federal grants for welfare.

Public assistance remains a politically charged issue. The most basic question it involves, however, relate to the views that society holds of poor and vulnerable people—including how they shall be supported—and the complex social and economic problems public-assistance recipients reflect, as well as the degree to which society will tolerate poverty amid plenty.

Religion

Christianity was one of the things that whites did not prohibit blacks from participating in. However in earlier years, even though they shared the same belief, blacks were not allowed to worship with whites. This should emphasize how strongly racism was rooted in the white community. Usually when people are of the same faith and practice the same religious doctrine, there is harmony and agreement. One would think that this would have been the one area that race would not have been such a factor. But because of white's attitude of supremacy, they would not allow blacks to worship in the same building. Many felt that Christianity was a religion for whites only and that blacks should be grateful that they were allowed to practice it at all. However there were those who felt that since blacks were a lessor human being, Christianity would teach them morals and the fear of hell and damnation would also provide another means of control. Most whites made it very clear to blacks that it was white people that God made in his own image and many whites are convinced in their minds that God is white. The pictures and images we are accustomed to of

Jesus, depict him with white skin, blonde hair and blue eyes, and since he is supposed to be the son of God, one would then conclude that God is white. Most blacks were raised practicing Christianity with these same images and in their minds have probably concluded or believe that God is white.

This belief system has given whites a superior attitude of self, while at the same time has given blacks an inferior attitude of themselves. There are blacks who have concluded that maybe God does favor whites, since in America they seem to live a happier and less stressful life than blacks. One must sometime wonder why so many blacks continue to practice Christianity if it seems to favor whites. It must be confusing to some as to why some whites who profess to be Christians can direct so much hate and racism against blacks, especially when most blacks in America consider themselves to be Christians also. Could it be that whites do not see blacks as an equal even if their religious beliefs are the same?

RACE RELATIONS IN THE MILITARY

The racial problems of the military today grew from and are in part shaped by the past. How racial minorities were treated by the army in the past, usually reflected the treatment of racial minorities in the US society as a whole. Race related attitudes and Behavior of soldiers today are frequently influenced by their image of history which in the area of race is often distorted, incomplete and inaccurate.

Despite the death of Crispus Attucks in the Boston, Massacre in 1775 and the participation of dozens of blacks in early battles, on November 12, 1775 General Washington, motivated partially by prejudice and fear of arming blacks issued an order instructing recruiters not to enlist blacks. The British Army eagerly welcomed freed blacks and run away slaves forcing the American Army to modify its position. Owners were given bounties to provide slaves for the duration of the war and slaves turned soldiers were promised freedom and their masters compensated at the going rate. At this time integration in the army was virtually complete.

In 1812 blacks had an opportunity once more to serve, but the numbers were small. There seemed to be no serious objections, but there was little inclination to recruit blacks. If slaves enlisted with the permission of their masters they were to receive their freedom at the duration of the war.

From the very beginning of the Civil war, northern blacks begged to enlist and were refused. It was not until abolition became inseparably linked with the restoration of the Union that the North considered raising black troops. After 1862 free blacks and emancipated slaves played a vital role in the Union war effort. More than 200,000 blacks in separate units fought and more than 38,000 lost their lives. When the South was having difficulty getting men for its armies, General Lee was in favor of enlisting blacks, but Jefferson Davis was opposed.

After the war, black men were called to fight red men in the West and still not convinced of the blacks soldiers ability, white men in Washington made it difficult as possible. The same inequalities which existed in civilian life manifested and magnified themselves in the army.

As late as World War I blacks were barred altogether from the marines and permitted to serve in the navy only, in the menial capacities. In the Army however, they served in nearly every branch, although, in segregated units. During World War II discrimination in the services still kept pace with civilian life. On July 26, 1948 President Harry s. Truman signed Executive Order 9981 that said in part:

> "There shall be equality of treatment and opportunity for all persons in the Armed

Forces without regard to race, color, religion
or national origin."

The order also established the President's Committee
on Equality of Treatment and Opportunity in the Armed
Forces to examine the rules, procedures and practices to
determine which should be altered or improved. Detailed
proposals for ending racial segregation were required from
each service. From this point integration proceeded slowly
but deliberately. In 1951 there were 200,000 black soldiers
serving in 385 all black units, by September, 1953 at the
end of the Korean War, only 88 all black units remained
in the army, accounting for only five percent of the black
enlisted men. Ironically, although blacks are now freely
accepted in the American Armed Forces, they are still
faced with discrimination at many levels. In 1966 there
were 22,000 blacks in Vietnam, some fifteen percent of
the total US commitment there. During that year 22 ½
% of all army troops killed in action were black. These
statistics suggest two things, first, since blacks composed
only ten percent of the total American population. There
were proportionately more blacks in the service than in
civilian life and second, a greater number of blacks than
whites were being sent to combat and dangerous zones.

Policy, Program, and Procedures in Race Relations.

Policy verses Reality:
Army Regulation 600-21,1965
  "It is the policy of the army to conduct all of
  its activities in a manner which is free from
  racial discrimination and which provides equal

> opportunity and treatment of all uniformed members irrespective of their race, color, religion or national origin."

Brigadier General George S. Patton

> "You show me a commander or a leader who says he doesn't have race trouble, and I'll show you a dumb son of a bitch."

The first quotation states the Army's fundamental policy with regard to race, this has been the policy for many years. The second quotation says something about the reality of race relations in the Army today, suggesting that policy may not yet be the reality. Although policy states goals of freedom from racial discrimination and equality of opportunity and treatment. The reality is that despite the Army's efforts to change, there continues to be real racial problems and racial discrimination still persists.

The Army has initiated programs to assist leaders in understanding the root causes of race problems. A typical unit in the Army includes individuals from a wide variety of backgrounds, from tenant farms, and ghettos, to middle class suburbs. Commands are encouraged to nurture an ever-growing sensitivity to feelings, desires and opinions of all. There is a strongly held view that leaders in the Army are color blind and do not see skin color, they only see green. This expression refers to the only color they see is the green uniform and race makes no difference to them. But many facts do not support this view. If it were true it would not be possible to show systematic correlation's between color of a man's skin and what happens to him in the Army. But, as with any other organization in American society, it is easy to show that such relationships do exist. The most obvious example is, of course, the bottom ranks are disproportionately filled with minorities, with minorities becoming more and more rare in the top ranks. In 1965 the Army was approximately fourteen percent black, with 3.6 percent black officers, in 1974 with 22 percent black there were still less than 4 percent black officers. Although this fact is now considerably less true in the Army today than in the other services and less true than it was only a few years ago, it is still true to a degree. Similarly, minorities are underrepresented in those highly technical jobs which have high economic value in the civilian world, and over-represented in jobs requiring only unskilled labor. Black soldiers are twice as likely as white soldiers to receive non-judicial punishment and courts martial convictions for direct confrontation experiences. There is a growing frequency with which black soldiers receive "bad paper," discharges, which are general, undesirable, bad conduct and dishonorable. According to black veterans organizations, of the estimated 20,000 bad paper discharges for which they are seeking reconsideration, fewer than a dozen have been reversed by the military.

Race Relations and the Leader

The army has made a commitment to solve its race problems. While it is perfectly clear that the Army cannot independently eliminate racial discrimination throughout the total society, it is clear that eliminating racial discrimination in the Army will mean that practices and actions which operate within the army to produce damaging, racially related effects will have to be changed.

The army tells its leaders that individuals operation in a harmful and racially discrimination manner will have to change their policies and actions. Unfortunately the very changes which will lower racial tensions by reducing the frustration of minority members have at the same time stimulated the so-called backlash charges of "reverse racism." What people usually refer to by the term, "reverse racism," are practices which appear to give preference and privilege to minorities. But in order to correct the harmful effect of past discrimination it is sometimes necessary to take special actions with respect to minority members in the present until such times as the harmful effects are corrected. If the scales are unbalanced, adding equal weights to both sides will never balance them. The late president Lyndon Johnson once expressed this idea in a compelling analogy in a speech at Howard University in 1965:

> "You do not take a person who, for years, has been hobbled by chains and liberate him, bring him up to a starting line of a race, and then say 'you are free to compete with all others' and still justly believe that you have been completely fair. Thus it is not enough to open the gates to opportunity. All of our citizens must have the ability to walk through those gates."

There has been a real effort to implement changes in such a way that the white majority will understand and accept the changes, the race relations seminars and training programs have been of real value. The broad purpose of the Army's Race Relations Education Program (RREP) is, "to promote racial harmony there by reducing racial tension and contributing directly to increased unit effectiveness." The specific goal of the program is to, "achieve sympathetic understanding and treatment of each soldier by his commanders and his fellows." The method used to accomplish this involves two separate elements; formal instructions in the Army schools, and participatory exchange of ideas on the history background, life styles and contributions of ethnic and racial minorities in unit seminars. One of the strengths of the Army Race Relations Training Program, is that it is an integral part of the Armies overall Race Relations/Equal Opportunity (RR/EE) effort. The program is designed to provide education for everyone-minority members, majority members and the leadership structure. The goal is to provide an understanding of the racial problem, and then to find ways of solving the problems. The Army views this education program as a Commander's Program designed to support him and his unit and therefore requiring his personal attention and direction.

Since the inception of the Army's RR/EP training is given to all active duty personnel, officers and enlisted, including reservist on active duty for training. In order to comply with the desires of the Secretary of Defense that equal opportunity programs be institutionalized as a priority management function, the Army had a complete reassessment of its race relations education effort. As a result it has developed the concept of an expanded wide program, with a view to insure comprehensive treatment of the subject on a continuing basis at all levels. The program integrates formal instruction in race relations given in the training establishment with a comprehensive program to improve interracial communication, called the Racial Awareness Program (RAP) in Army units. To insure that top managers and leaders are sufficiently sensitive to the problem of racial tension and the methods of countering it, they are given special training. RAP includes all unit activities directed toward improving interracial communication. Mandatory race relations seminars are the cornerstone of the program. Also included are such military and civilian activities as, "Black History month, the observance of significant calendar events, and unit race relations conferences. The seminars are conducted in every unit in the army, the program devotes time to subjects such as prejudice, minority and majority stereotypes, the feelings of minorities and those of majorities, the contributions of minorities to American life, the life styles of both, eliminating institutional racism in the unit, racial issues facing the Nation and the unit, and combating discrimination.

Commanders are given lists of typical complaints that should be investigated thoroughly. Degrading treatment by individuals, the most common form of this complaint is about abusive language. Discrimination in selection procedures. Inadequate on post facilities, off-post discrimination injustice in the justice system, racial favoritism, inoperative grievance system, are just a few of the many complaints.

The Army is correcting many problems. In 1971, major policy changes were announced by the Secretary of the Army. Commanders were authorized to impose restrictive sanctions against any rental facility whose owner or manager was found to be discriminating on the basis of race, and Housing Referral Offices were established Army wide to insure that soldiers did not rent from discriminating landlords; changes were made to the non-judicial punishment procedures which were designed to lessen the chances of racial discrimination and to protect the rights of individual soldiers; minority group representation was required on all promotion boards, and the Army sent participants to the first class of the Department of Defense's Race Relations Institute in Florida. In 1972, an Equal Opportunity Race Relations Affirmative Action Plan had been formally approved, the plan set forth both short and long range goals and represents the most comprehensive program yet developed for ensuring equal opportunity and treatment for all.

All sizable installations have military equal opportunity staff personnel consisting of officers and NCO's. These individuals serve as a point of contact, where soldiers may express racial grievances they might not otherwise reveal. In addition they assist the command in planning and monitoring race relations programs, implementing policies and giving advice and assistance in racial matters at all levels. They are also charged with developing and monitoring local command and staff developed Affirmative Action Plans. Many installations have established Race Relations Councils. Their functions are to serve as a forum for discussing racial matter, evaluate progress and the effectiveness of the race relations program and submit recommendations to the commander for consideration and action. They identify and recommend establishment of priorities for specific projects and tasks requiring consultant services not available in the Department of the Army. The councils also plan and conduct seminars, educational programs, and workshops as needed.

Under present plans, the Army's entire effort is devoted to increasing inter-racial communication and improving racial harmony. That adds up to many man hours per year focused on the Army's race relations. In terms of the individual, every soldier receives continuous exposure to race relations for his or her entire period of service. Sol Stern wrote in the New York Times on March 24, 1968:

> "If lack of skills and education drive young blacks into the Army in the first place, the military could turn out to be a contributor of social equality in civilian life. By providing vocational training that blacks would otherwise not receive, the army could send back men qualified for jobs to reduce the number of hard corps unemployed. On the other hand, the military teaches men to lead in combat situations, if ghetto conditions do not improve, if equal opportunity is not forthcoming the black ex-soldier provide excellent material for combat leadership in the cities." The Army with its myriad of cultural and social backgrounds is facing a new urgency to resolve problems of race relations. Neither the Army nor the Nation can afford under utilization of minority

soldiers and certainly they cannot endure combat units with a significant number of hostile or alienated soldiers.

For over two hundred years the black soldier has fought for his own personal freedom as well as for his country. It is no longer a question of proving ability; the black soldier has proved his heroism. Today the issues are acceptance as a human being, an American citizen and being granted the dignity and the privileges those identities imply. The military seems to have made great progress in the area of race relations. They have a plan and insist of total involvement by all their personnel. Of course no organization can regulate individual thinking, but organizations can insist on certain standard of behavior while one is participating in the functions of the organization. The leadership of organizations and institutions musts let it be known that acts of discrimination or discriminatory behavior of any kind, will not be tolerated. This will cause participants to adjust their behavior accordingly. Having to adjust ones behavior on a daily basis, sometimes causes one to change their thinking on some issues. This is the kind of policy implementation that has helped the military to minimize racial problems. It is difficult to totally eradicate it, because of the preconceived ideas many bring from civilian life, and are able to mask their true feelings about race.

Another major aspect of the military's success in race relations is formal education. The military supports and encourages its members to increase their education. This is promoted at all levels and it is rewarded by promotions and greater responsibility. Attaining more education always enhances an individual's self-esteem. Education often exposes one to new ways of thinking about old ideas, and a new way of solving problems.

Reverse Discrimination

Today there are some whites, mostly white males complaining of reverse discrimination. They complain that some blacks on certain jobs are being promoted ahead of them even though the black person may some time have less time on the job than they and some say with less qualification. Those complaining feel this is so unjust, even though the number of whites who experience this is very small. They seem to forget that a whole race of people have been experiencing this for a very long time. These same white people have been receiving special advantages and privileges for a very long time. Blacks and other minorities were being totally denied employment in many places and only allowed to work in certain positions if they were hired. They could only advance so far no matter what their qualifications were. They were only allowed to live in certain areas and often charged more for certain basic necessities. While all of this was accepted practice, none of those now complaining ever considered it unfair or unjust that blacks and other minorities were being treated this way. Most felt that blacks and other minorities did not deserve to be treated the same or have the same economic status as white people. The justification for this special treatment was that they were white. It did not matter that the minorities were good hard working people. Good citizens and tax payers. Now that some whites in power have agreed that it is now time to try to make up for some of the systematic racism and discrimination that is perpetrated against minorities. So the government passes an affirmative action plan, which is designed to provide minorities an opportunity to try and catch up to where they should be in employment and in education. Many companies in the past had refused to hire blacks or other minorities, even though they were a large segment of the population in the areas where they were located. These companies hired minorities and after a few years it was necessary to move some into higher positions. This meant that some minorities would have to be promoted ahead of some white workers who may have had more time on the job. One has to remember that the minorities did not have the same amount of time on the job because years before the company refused to hire them at all. There was no other way for a company to try and balance the scale. So what some are calling reverse discrimination, is really corrective action of an unfair and unjust practice based solely on race. It is also very strange that the accusation of reverse discrimination by a few white people, get more attention and publicity than the charge of racism in general by all minorities. Also in the past it was whites discrimination against blacks and other minorities and in the case of the whites complaining, it is not blacks who are discriminating against the whites, so how can it be reverse?

No-Respect

There seem to be some white Americans who feel that black Americans are not worthy of respect. There are many who seem to think black American and other minorities can be the brunt of their jokes and disrespected. It seems that whites with a superior attitude do not and will never see black Americans and other non white minorities as an equal.

There are many white Americans who ridicule black Americans at the expense of loosing their jobs or positions of authority.

According to a Washington Post article titled May 2 Specified in Hate Letter; Georgetown Students warned. Georgetown University received a hate letter stating that on May 2 African American Students should "Look Out." A university official stated "The University will not tolerate acts of hatred and threatened violence." The point is at this late date why would anyone be making racial threats on a university campus. We should be over that kind of action against black Americans and other minorities.

Its as though some people cannot help making racial remarks against black people as though they do not deserve any respect. Many act as though black Americans being equal is a joke.

Another Washington Post Article in 1999, title Navy Officer Calls His Dismissal From Training Racial Bias. The article also stated that no black officer has ever completed the residency program. A Cmdr. who was stationed there at the time stated that other staff members in the prosthondontics department described the black officer, behind his back as "Cmdr. – and joking about his big fat black [behind]."

The Cmdr. who was trying to defend the black officer, said, that one staff member stated, "The bottom line is, do we really want his kind to be in our specialty?"

Before coming to Bethesda the black officer was highly regarded.

The board of five (5) officers rejected the black officer's appeal.

The board acknowledged that "insensitivity may exist" at the school and said that the issue merits further study."

It seems that some white people cannot resist making racial comments about black people. Even though it may cost them their job or position of authority.

Recently in the Washington DC Metropolitan area. A very popular radio personality was suspended for referring to a young black women's basketball team, as nappy headed whores, as a joke. This happened in 2007.

There are some white Americans who even commit crimes, expressing their negative racial attitudes. In Maryland, some new homes were set fire, because some black American had signed contracts to purchase some of these homes.

If all Americans would respect Americans that are different than themselves, we would be a stronger nation. We must learn to embrace out diversity. Everyone deserves Respect and the right to enjoy the many benefits of our great country.

CONCLUSION

This writing has been addressed mainly to the black and white racial problem, but because of the belief in white supremacy by some white Americans, all people of color are discriminated against by a large segment of the white population and many of our institutions.

It appears that black Americans are the targets of the most vehement acts of discrimination. Only negative images of them are shown in the media most of the time. They are harassed more often than others by law enforcement, treated unfairly by businesses, regarding credit and service in general and in employment and advancement. Black Americans are denied most of the privileges that make white Americans proud to be citizens of the United States. It is my belief that if we ever reach a point in the country, where black Americans are treated fairly and with the respect that white Americans feel they deserve, the problems of all other so called minorities will also be resolved.

White American's reaction to a trial verdict is indicative of how they view black Americans. White Americans assumed that the mostly black jury reached its decision on emotion rather than an evaluation of the evidence. This alone is very insulting to black people. It infers that they are incapable of rendering a just and fair verdict, when the defendant is black. Nothing is farther from the truth, because in many places throughout the country, black judges, black prosecutors and juries are convicting black criminals everyday, and have no problems or conflict about it.

If an individual has a behavior problem such as alcoholism or drug addition, we often hear that they can not be helped, unless they first admit they have a problem. Maybe that is one reason very little is done about racism in America, because most white Americans are unwilling to admit that we have a problem. Once we admit there is a problem, then blacks and whites can begin to work together to rid ourselves of this detrimental practice. We must deal with it or eventually no one in the country will have a true pursuit of happiness. We should not continue passing this terrible behavior to our children. Many whites become very defensive about racism, they feel it began before their time and therefore they are not responsible for it. That may be true somewhat, but they are responsible and guilty of perpetuating it. We must be concerned about the effect racism has on the country as a whole.

It is amazing that most white Americans deny being racist. Most resent the topic being discussed, because it makes them uncomfortable. There are many who really don't believe there is a problem of race. They have conditioned themselves to believe that things are as they should be. They are convinced that the problems faced by blacks and other minorities are caused by themselves and not by white America. They fail to realize that this kind of thinking exemplify the attitude of white supremacy.

Whites are not aware of how their actions affects blacks. It lowers their self esteem and can have devastating effects on the way some react to society as a whole. It is very difficult to maintain a high opinion of ones self, when you are treated negatively in almost every aspect of your life, your job, business, socially and law enforcement. It is a baffling situation, because we live in a country that boast about its Christian morals and values, and yet so many dislike and treat people negatively simply because they are a different color.

As Americans we are fortunate to live in the greatest country in the world. The country has survived many problems and adversities, economical, political, and several wars. Because of the patriotism of all its citizens and unity during difficult times, the country has always remained strong and the envy of the rest of the world. That is why it is so puzzling, that we allow the forces of racism and bigotry to continue to divide the country and prevent us from becoming even greater than we are as a nation.

We all must let it be known that prejudging or treating a person negatively solely because of race is unacceptable behavior in this society. It must be understood that none of us can be totally free if some of us are held back because of a circumstance over which they have no control; their race.

Most people agree that what happened to Jewish people in Germany during World War II was a terrible crime. We all agree that all people of the world should do everything possible to insure that such a crime never happens again to any people. We are constantly reminded by the Jewish population of this tragic event. They want to be sure that we learn from this history and that we never forget. This allows those who are too young to know what happened, be aware of the evil nature of prejudice and discrimination and the devastating effect it has on the victims of it.

It is rather baffling that many white Americans seem to want the history of racism and discrimination and the effect it has had on black people to just be forgotten. Many seem to be in a state of denial. They don't seem to understand how devastating the acts of slavery, discrimination and prejudice have been for black Americans. We as a people must look upon what has happened to blacks in America with the same compassion and concern that we feel for the Jewish population. We must also make sure that our young people know what happened and how it happened, so that we may better understand the problem and why it has no place in American society.

We cannot change or deny what happened, but we can learn from it, and maybe understand why some of us react the way we do with one another. It is sad, because the racism in America is based solely on skin color. Many of the Caucasian people in America come from varied ethnic backgrounds, but most see themselves as one race and based on skin color alone they are more privileged and respected than others in the country.

Many of our young white Americans don't understand why blacks and other minority groups complain about discrimination. They don't seem to wonder why things are so much better for them than for those of a different color. Maybe its because they have bought into the myth of white supremacy, and do not understand that instead it is white control. Maybe its because many have no real knowledge of our past history regarding race. Their parents want to forget it and therefore do not insure that their children understand the history of racism in America. It just may be that once they understand, they may want no part in perpetuating this sickness in our society. This is another reason that books that reflect on how things were in the past, should not be removed from libraries or class rooms. It must be discussed and seen as something that has no place in a diverse society such as ours. We might fight for the freedom of all our citizens and understand that there is strength in our diversity. We can change our future of tomorrow, if we are willing to change our thinking of today.

For those who just do not seem to understand how unfairly blacks have been treated even in the military while fighting for their country. The recent awarding of medals to black soldiers for service in World War II. These soldiers were denied this honor during and right after the war for no other reason, except they were black. There were 432 medals of honor presented for World War II service. There were none presented to blacks even though more than one million served in that war. It was accepted practice that no black soldier would receive the military's highest award, no matter how exemplary their service was. This was outrageous and Americans should be ashamed that they ever allowed a practice such as this. It is my hope that this kind of behavior by our military is a thing of the past and that our citizens would not permit anything of this nature today.

White Americans in the past have committed discriminating acts and practices with impunity. It seemed that all white Americans agreed with such actions. Most often white Americans never complain about unfair treatment of blacks and other minorities, in schools, the workplace, the justice system and even in religious institutions. Many white clergymen never used their pulpits to try and change the attitude of their congregations or ask that they at least not condone the discriminating practices of others. This was probably due to the fear of losing members of their congregation or of being ostracized themselves. Once again no one wants to accept responsibility for racism and discrimination nor does anyone want to accept the responsibility of trying to eradicate the practice.

There is a saying that if you place a bucket under a leaking faucet, it will be fine for a while, but once the bucket is full it runs over. The bucket of seeing some in our society have so much, while others have so little and no hope of ever changing their situation is almost full and if nothing is done it will run over. The resentment will continue to build and no one can predict what the outcome may be.

Because racism is so prevalent in the society and those in power don't see a potential for a serious class revolution, nothing is done to relieve the pressure that those at the bottom are forced to live with. There must be things done to enable blacks and other minorities to improve their economic status.

There is a problem with blacks who have played by the rules and have done those things that society dictate that one must do to become economically successful and they are still far below their white counterparts. There is no explanation for this except racism. They are still limited as to how much they can earn and earning much less than some whites with less education and training. This kind of behavior cannot continue forever, although some whites see no problem. This is also not a good incentive for younger blacks and other minorities to further their education if they see those before them not reaping any significant benefit from doing so.

Some young people are developing relationships with people of different races and backgrounds, but many of their parents object to these relationships without any real basic except race. Many do it out of fear because they have never had relationships with blacks or other minorities and have only stereotypical images not based on fact, to draw from. This makes them appear as racist, which may be true in some cases but in many, its a fear of the unknown. They do not know how to unlearn the erroneous information they have received about people of other races.

It is obvious that improvements have been made during the past 40 years. Yet there are still some white people who believe they should have more priviledges and opportunities than non-white citizens. This is a belief that has been passed on from one generation to the next as though it is an inheritance.

Many white parents are still teaching their children white supremacy, and instilling in them the notion that they are special and therefore entitled to more priviledges and opportunities, simply because they are white. This attitude breeds contempt and anger among the non-white population. All citizens make the same contributions. All races have served in our military, we all pay taxes to provide our government the revenue it needs to operate, and non-white citizens are as patriotic as white citizens are. There are some among us who will not allow the country to be cured of this sickness, so that we may work toward unifying our citizens, so that we may become a stronger nation. We all must work hard to rid our country of this problem or it may be the fire within that will detroy us.

There are whites, blacks and other minorities in our society who are working together, living together and doing just fine. These people have gotten to know one another and have found that they have more in common than differences. They have also learned that they are not really at odds with each other, but are divided by attitudes that keep them from relating in positive ways.

Racism is so inherent in American society, that most whites don't see it as the destructive power that it is. Whites in different parts of the country react almost identical to a similar situation regarding race. This is because they receive basically the same orientation from the institutions that is so much a part of their lives. Although racism is in all of American society, no one wants to acknowledge it or accept responsibility for its perpetuation.

Many younger white Americans want to distance themselves from todays racism. They see it as something of and from the past. They fail to realize that unless they acknowledge the wrongs commutted in the past, they will not be able to find adequate solutions for todays racial problems. It is not something that can just be ignored. It must be openly and honestly dealt with.

It is very difficult to motivate young people living in a racist society. It is especially difficult for black parents, who try to give their children positive attitudes about racial situations. Often they are being subjected to negative and unfair treatment by the majority of society. Many lose hope and give up because they see no positive future for themselves. People can no longer say, the problem of discrimination is "their" problem, because it is everyones problem. The negative effects of this type of attitude effects us all. Young black people are not rewarded for their positive actions and behavior. Racism destroys the spirit of people and their hope that anything they do will make a difference in how they are treated.

There is a need for changing how we think about certain situations, and educate ourselves about those who are different than we are. We may then find that except for race, we are very much the same in so many other ways. We may also come to the conclusion, that we are all Americans who love our country. We then can work together to make it a better place to live and raise our children. Most Americans want to participate in any efforts to make our country better. They do not wish to be excluded.

Racism destroys the victims by the way they are treated and it also eventually destroy those who perceive themselves as superior.

The solutions to racism is really in the heart and mind of individuals, therefore we must start with ourselves and our own families.

Bibliography:

Combs, Michael, and Gruhl, Johns, eds., Affirmative Action: Theory, Analysis, and Prospects (1986); Schwartz, B., Beyond Bakke (1988); Walter, M.A., and Block, W., eds., Discrimination, Affirmative Action, and Equal Opportunity (1982).

Copyrights – 1992 Grolier Electronic Publishing, Inc.

Bibliography: Allport, Gordon W., The Nature of Prejudice (1954); Bettelheim, Bruno, and Janowitz, Morris, Social Change and Prejudice (1964); Dovidio, J.D., and Gaertner, S.L., Prejudice, Discrimination, and Racism (1986); Simpson, G.E., and Yinger, J.M., Racial and Cultural Minorities: An Analysis of Prejudice and Discrimination, 5th ed. (1985).

(History)   The Negro in American History (Wm Loren Katz)

              Black Power, by S. Carmichael & C. Hamilton Vintage 1967

(Society)   Institutional Racism in America
              Developing New Perspectives on Race
              Grolier Electronic Publishing, Inc.

Washington Post News Paper Articles

Coughlin, R.M., ed., Reforming Welfare: Lessons, Limits, and Choices (1989); Danziger, S.H., and Weinberg,

D.H., eds., Fighting Poverty: What Works and What Doesn't (1986); DiNitto, Diana M., et al., Social Welfare, 2nd ed. (1987); Dolgoff, R.L., and Feldstein, Donald, Understanding Social Welfare, 2nd ed. (1986); Gilbert, Neil, et al., Dimensions of Social Welfare Policy, 2nd ed. (1986); Gronbjerg, K.A., Mass Society and the Extension of Welfare, 1960-1970 (1977), handler, J.F., and Sosin, Michael, Last resorts: Emergency Assistance and Special Needs Programs in Public Welfare (1983); Johnson, Harriette, and Goldberg, Gertrude, Government Money for Everyday People (1982); Levitan, S.A., Orograms in Aid of the Poor for the 1980's 3rd ed. (1986); Mead, L.M., Beyond Entitlement: The Social Obligations of Citizenship (1985); Murray, Charles, Losing ground: American Social Policy, 1950-1980 (1984); Piven F.F., and Cloward, R.A., Regulating the Poor: The Functions of Public Welfare (1971); Sherraden, Michael, Assets and the Poor: A New American Welfare Policy (1991).

About the Author

H. Marcel Evans was born in Birmingham, Alabama. His family later moved to Cleveland, Ohio. He served twenty years in the military service. After serving in Vietnam, he became an Instructor of Equal Opportunity and Race Relations, as one of his assigned duties. H. Marcel presently lives in Northern Virginia, with his wife, Zenobia, and daughters, Robin and Ronda. He also has three sons, Randall, Rami and Andre and another daughter Marcelles.